UNPACKING
AGAPE

The 7 Languages Of Intentional Leadership

Dawn Marie Morris

BOOK BONUS INSIDE!

Take the quiz to determine your most organic

Agape Leadership Language!

Table of Contents

UNPACKING 1
AGAPE 1
The 7 Languages Of Intentional Leadership 1
Table of Contents 3
PRELUDE 1
THE INTENTIONAL LEADERSHIP MODEL 5
THE INTENTIONAL LEADER 14
    An Intentional Leader Motivates to Win 20
    An Intentional Leader's Behaviors Show That You Matter 23
LEADERSHIP AND ITS CONNECTION TO LOVE 28
    Agape Love in Leadership 30
    Agape Love as an Intentional Leader 31
    Agape Love-A Basis of Servant Leadership 36
The Languages of Agape Leadership 39
    What are the Languages of Agape Leadership? 43
    Agape Leadership Language #1: 45
    Agape Leadership Language #1: 46
    Ambassador of Forgiveness 46
    Agape Leadership Language #2: 49
    Carrier of Ethics 49
    Agape Leadership Language #3: 53
    Team Leader of Tenacity 53

    Agape Leadership Language #4: 58
    Caretaker of Temperance 59
    Agape Leadership Language #5: 64
    Relentless Visionary 64
    Agape Leadership Language #6: 68
    Never Beyond Approach 68
    Agape Leadership Language #7: 72
    Steward of "The Ship" 72
The Distinctions 75
    Distinction #1: Heightened Team Comradery 76
    Distinction #2: Stronger Results 77
    Distinction #3: The Minimization of Stress 78
    Distinction #4: The "Light" is Undeniable 80
A Closing Love Letter 84
    Dear Leaders: 85
BONUS: 87
What's Your Primary Agape Leadership Language? 87
ABOUT DAWN MARIE MORRIS 102

PRELUDE

Intentionality, Intention, Leading with Intention...these words have become very commonplace in our society. Yet, not much exists on what being intentional like. What behaviors does a person who exhibits intentionality display?

Is it demonstrated by early arrival to a job, an event, or another commitment?

Is it demonstrated by honoring one's word or communicating fully the reason that one's word is not honored?

Is it taking the time to pay attention to the details of a task, ensuring that one leaves no parts unattended?

Is it drawing into the depths of one's energy when it seems like the task is too daunting or taking too long?

I submit that intentionality, and for purposes of this book, leading with intention, causes us to draw on all these behaviors, sometimes individually and at other times, collectively.

Webster derives intention from the root word, intent, which means "resolved or determined to do." As intentional leaders, we demonstrate resolve to influence well when we act in a manner that encapsulates the title of this book, L-O-V-E.

AGAPE: The Language of Intentional Leadership will help you to uncover how to let those whom you influence know that you have resolved and determined to lead them well.

Through this book, you will also discover the agape leadership love language that is most organic for you to demonstrate. As a leader, it will be important that you lean into that love language as you build strength in the others.

SECTION 1

INTENTIONAL LEADERSHIP EXPLAINED

THE ROLE OF SERVANT LEADERSHIP IN INTENTIONAL LEADERS

A servant leader, one who operates from a place of agape love, selfless, sacrificial care, and concern for others, is indeed one who demonstrates the seven love languages of an intentional leader. It is impossible to be a servant leader and not use the agape languages.

In the pages of this book lie a deeper discovery of the behaviors that are representative of agape. These behaviors will also be referred to as languages. This will be explained shortly.

Before we delve more into agape language in leadership, it is key that we explore what it means to be an intentional leader.

Let us begin by defining The Intentional Leadership Model.

THE INTENTIONAL LEADERSHIP MODEL

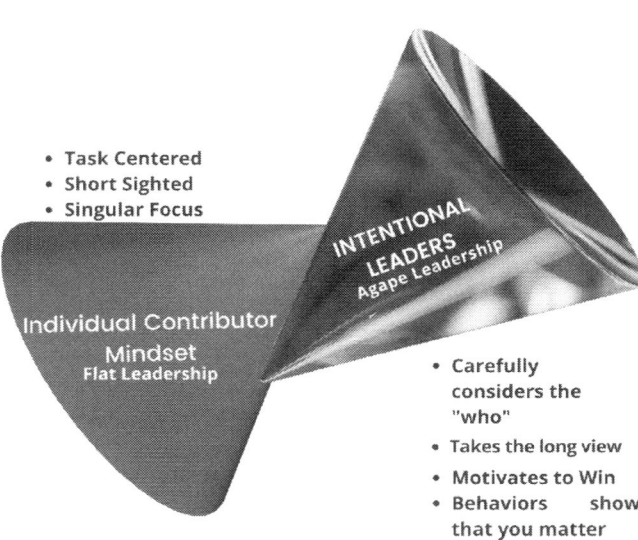

The Intentional Leadership Model emphasizes the depth of the leader who operates from a place of sacrificial leadership, juxtaposed with the "flat" style of the leader who has an individual contributor mindset.

The Individual Contributor Mindset

When a leader moves into positions of authority, their first emergence is typically from a place of high producing individual contributor. In these instances, the person was heralded for being a "task master." Because of demonstrated proficiency in completing assignments, they received a promotion to a leader of people. While this can appear like a great move, the challenge arises if the mindset of the leader does not shift from task master, or "individual contributor," to "intentional leader."

Let us dissect the "Individual Contributor Mindset."

AGAPE

"Only a life lived in service to others is worth living."

ALBERT EINSTEIN

THE INDIVIDUAL CONTRIBUTOR MINDSET

- Task Centered
- Short Sighted
- Singular Focus

At this level, the mindset focuses on the tasks that they are to complete each day, week, month, or year. The leader measures the individual contributor by how well the individual contributor meets his or her task-related goals. This is not to say that one or two "people-centered" discussions do not come into play. However, the primary determinants of success or failure lie at the task level.

Employees who are excellent individual contributors have more of a myopic view of the organization. Their sphere of influence is limited, in most cases, to those with whom they interact most frequently. While this can create a level of comfort and sense of security, it can deter human skills growth necessary to achieve success in leadership.

An individual contributor who is seeking to expand his or her influence within the organization must employ, as one tool, systems thinking.

What is "systems thinking"?

One definition by Dr. Marie Morganelli, a freelance content writer and editor at Precise Words Creative, states in an article that she drafted for Southern New Hampshire University that systems thinking is, **"a holistic way to investigate factors and interactions that could contribute to a possible outcome."**[1] (Morganelli, 2020)

Dr. Morganelli goes on to say that systems thinking helps team members to take a deeper look at how they resolve problems and create change by considering key stakeholders, complementary

---

[1] Dr. Marie Morganelli, "What is Systems Thinking?" *https://www.snhu.edu/about-us/newsroom/business/what-is-systems-thinking*, Southern New Hampshire University, March 18, 2020.

departments, and other factors.

As Dr. Morganelli went on to share, "systems thinking is not about winning a battle or being right." Systems thinking allows those who are at the table to take the long view and consider several options and outcomes when planning or deciding.

Systems thinking requires leaders to think outside of their immediate department and what is best for them. Often, great leaders will enlist the opinions of key constituents in other departments before implementing a change or deciding. This serves two purposes. One is that it builds relationships. Strong interdepartmental communication helps to breed cooperation. The second is that it allows the leader who is considering or planning a change to gain insight and perspective from another viewpoint. It is like looking at a forest from both sides of the same tree. Standing on one side may only give you sight of the buildings. Standing on the other side gives you sight of the water. Standing on both sides allows you to fully explain the entire view.

An individual contributor who resists the need to engage

systems thinking is sure to limit organizational reach.

Human Skills Development

The other big developmental need for those going from individual contributor to intentional leader is human skills. To highlight how this appears, I will share a recent story that I heard about an employee who received a promotion after over 20 years at one company. (NOTE: The names and company are different.)

Reda had been working at Institute A88 for over 20 years. During her tenure as a manager, her store's profit and loss numbers were phenomenal. Reda worked at the same store for over 15 years and knew everyone there very well. However, she was abrupt and short with the team members. While she was abrupt and short in communication with her team members, her great store numbers kept her in remarkable favor with district leadership.

Reda interviewed for and received a promotion that took her away from the store and placed her on the corporate side. In this role, she interacted with team members across the country. Her leaders assessed her team's timeliness delivering and stocking the stores in her region. Her leaders also evaluated her team communication and development.

Because Reda had not expanded her view beyond her store for so many years, and they had put up with her poor communication skills (human skills), she struggled in her new role. Team members complained that she minimized the importance of the work that they had accomplished before she started. She used the same abrupt delivery that she was accustomed to making in the stores and hardly gave them an opportunity to speak and share their thoughts. It was her way or the highway! Also, she made changes without consulting anyone. Interdepartmental leadership was concerned because some of the changes that were not communicated to them impacted their team's operations.

You may be thinking, "Well, Reda was already a leader. Why was she not thinking as an intentional leader? Why did she have an individual contributor mindset?"

The problem is that, while Reda had already been a leader, or had the title associated with leadership (store manager), she still operated with an "Individual Contributor *Mindset*." Remember, being an intentional leader and being an individual contributor is not about position. Rather, it is about behavior.

Reda was in the mindset of an individual contributor. For years, her concern was about the success of her store. If it succeeded, her leaders celebrated her. This, for a company that has over 570 stores, is short-sighted, and is not the way to succeed when operating at the corporate level.

Reda needed to expand her sphere of influence by strengthening her human skills capacity.

How does one do that?

One becomes an "Intentional Leader."

Let us read more about the intentional leader.

THE INTENTIONAL LEADER

- Carefully considers the "who"
- Takes the long view
- Motivates to Win
- Behaviors show that you matter

Now that we have looked at the individual contributor mindset, let us look at the intentional leader.

Referencing our definition outlined in the earlier pages, Webster derives intention from the root word, intent, which means "resolved or determined to do. A supervisor, manager, director, or C-Suite executive who is an intentional leader, has determined to behave in a manner that:

- ✓ Carefully considers the "who"
- ✓ Takes the long view
- ✓ Motivates to win
- ✓ Demonstrates behaviors that show you (the teammates) matter

Let us explore each one.

An Intentional Leader Carefully Considers the Who

A person in position who has determined or resolved to lead well knows that having quality teammates is mission critical. Having a team member who is either capable, but not willing or willing, but not capable can be stressful, time-consuming, and can lead to client loss, money loss, and even legal issues. This is in the global sense.

On a task-by-task basis, an intentional leader needs to use careful consideration in delegation, as well. When delegating tasks, it is necessary to remember two things:

- The person to whom you delegate is RESPONSIBLE

- The intentional leader is ACCOUNTABLE

When delegating tasks, it is vital to keep in mind that when a leader selects someone to carry it out that they are holding that person responsible for what they may one day have to give an account.

Dear Leaders,

RESIST THE URGE TO TAKE A HANDS-OFF APPROACH TO TASKS THAT YOU DELEGATE!

Just because you have assigned it to someone else does not mean that you absolve yourself of the responsibility to know what is happening with that task. As an intentional leader your job is to:

- ✓ Ensure the person to whom the task is delegated has the skill and the will to complete it.
- ✓ Work together to agree on expectations
- ✓ Set follow-up times… **AND…** follow-up
- ✓ Provide support when needed
- ✓ Communicate to ensure the team member completes the task
- ✓ Debrief to uncover wins and opportunities for the next time

Always? **ALWAYS**.

An Intentional Leader Takes the Long View

Going back to our friend, Reda, who was the store superstar, but struggled when she received the promotion and went to the corporate level, if she were leading with intention, she would have taken the long view.

This view is the comprehensive view. It happens when the leader looks beyond their current situation, request, problem, or assignment. It may be considering 3 or 4 factors that caused a process to fail. It may be considering choosing 2 or 3 outcomes to an opportunity that is presented. It may be engaging with complementary departments to see what happens on their end when working with products you send them or requests that you submit. It may involve putting in place 1 or 2 backup plans in the event the original plan cannot be executed in the manner intended.

The long view is the systems thinking view.

Intentional leadership requires non-linear thinking. It requires that you study the business processes of other departments. Understanding how they operate may help you to streamline your operation, or better prepare for delays because you understand what happens on the other side. It also requires that you study other people. Study them, if possible, before you interact with them. Do not study with the intention of changing who you are to fit who they are. Study them with the intention of understanding how they think so that you can communicate in a way that drives positive interaction. Be your authentic self, but "seek first to understand, then to be understood."

If Reda had taken time to visit outside of her store before going to corporate so that she understood the culture and how they operated, it is likely that she would have had better initial interactions with her team members. Also, she would have been in a better position to make changes without pushback because the team would have recognized that she had studied them before she received the promotion.

Take the long view. It can appear slow, at times, but it can yield impressive results. As one writer said, *"Slow and steady wins the race."*

An Intentional Leader Motivates to Win

This principle may seem like common sense. However, it needs to be stated. Returning to our definition, the word intentional is derived from the root word intend, which means "resolved" or "determined to do." An intentional leader must be resolved or determined to WIN. The intentional leader needs to have a winning mindset and know how to motivate the team to want to win, as well.

What does this look like? The first thing one sees is ENERGY. An intentional leader who motivates to win exudes a certain energy that is infectious. When they show up, a metaphorical light goes on that says, "Let's get it!" The team feels this energy. It is not transferred through words alone.

The second indicator of an intentional leader who motivates to win is their response to difficult circumstances. In leadership there will be many challenges that are faced and overcome. The intentional leader who motivates to win finds a way to tap into the nature of the team in a way that causes them to either find a way to press through the challenge to victory or unpack a defeat in such a way that they find the pieces that will help them to win the next time. This person does not carry the weight of negative circumstances around like a badge of honor.

Recently, a Netflix documentary called, *The Playbook-A Coach's Rules for Life*, highlighted, among other notable coaches, Dawn Staley, head coach of the South Carolina Gamecocks. (Brentlinger, 2020) In her interview, she shared the pain of defeat that she carried with her in her NCAA Championship loss as a player at the University of Virginia. She said that she was unable to erase that feeling from her mind for some time after the loss. Eventually, however, she realized that she must shake it off to continue to move ahead. From that experience, she developed a mantra for her team of *24 Hours---From a Victory or From a Defeat--- They Let It Go and Move On.*[2]

As intentional leaders who motivate to win, letting go of the past is necessary to be victorious. 24 hours…to celebrate wins or sulk in defeat…then move ahead with intention!

---

[2] Brentlinger, Bryce. Henion, John. Staley, Dawn. (2020) *The playbook: A coach's rules for life* [motion picture] United States of America: Boardwalk Pictures, Dellrio Films, Springhill Entertainment.

The third way that an intentional leader motivates to win is by behavior. Are you demonstrating a winning work ethic? Are you accountable to your teammates? Are you supportive? Are you helping them to produce the best that they can? Are you fostering an environment that helps them to develop into winners?

People often become motivated when they see their leaders executing at an elevated level, in production, integrity, work ethic and support. It is important that your energy and your language match your behavior. Falling short in this area can make a world of difference in your ability to motivate to win. If you do not behave in a manner that is in line with your words, the team can become demotivated. Productivity and respect may suffer.

As an intentional leader who motivates to win you go first by being a winner.

AGAPE

"There is a difference between being a leader and being a boss. Both are based on authority. A boss demands blind obedience; a leader earns his authority through understanding and trust."

KLAUS BLAKENHOL

An Intentional Leader's Behaviors Show That You Matter

Two of the best leaders that I had in my corporate career did one thing that put them in a category by themselves...they demonstrated behaviors that signified that I mattered.

The first one we will call Linea. While working for Linea, I was told on a Wednesday by my direct manager that human resources wanted to talk to me on Friday. Having no idea why they wanted to have a conversation with me, I was nervous for two days.

Friday evening, while I was at home, they called and shared a litany of accusations that were clearly designed to railroad me. Fortunately, I took copious notes.

At the end of the conversation, I asked the human resources director what the result of the conversation was going to be. She said that she would tell me on Monday. Monday was not good enough for me.

Immediately following the call, I drafted an email to Linea, the VP of the department, and copied everyone who I thought needed to be in the loop. I outlined everything that was incorrect and suspect. I told them that I was taking the next two days off so that they could remedy this situation.

Here is where Linea showed that I mattered.

She called me and expressed her discontent with what had happened. She said, "I know that you are a rock star in the training room." She further insured me that there would be no actions taken and that I should feel comfortable returning to work.

Linea, who was two levels up, stepped in and stepped up. She let me know that I mattered to the team, something I will always remember.

The second of my best leaders we will call Dion. Dion did two things that separated him from the pack. One is quite simple. Every morning he arrived at work, he took a moment to stop by our desks and say, "Good morning." He did not rush into his office and go about his day as if we did not exist. No matter what lied ahead of him, he let us know that we were essential pieces of the team.

The other highlight of this leader surrounds an issue, as well. One of the employees in a department we worked with closely came to my desk and told me that I did not have authority to draft an email. I was the head of training and development at the time, and she was an HR systems person who had no authority to tell me that. Additionally, the way she approached me was unacceptable. She left her floor to come to my desk, approached me as if she were reprimanding me, asked me to leave my desk and demanded that I retract my email message. This was unconscionable!

When I expressed this to Dion, he did not brush off my concern as insignificant. Rather, he held a meeting with both of us and let her know that her behavior was unacceptable. I left the meeting knowing that I mattered to him. My concern mattered to him. I was an essential piece.

With both leaders it was their determination to let me know that my presence made a difference that made THE DIFFERENCE.

An intentional leader has instances that are innumerable to let team members know that they matter. Whether it is as simple as saying, "Good morning", as Dion did, or more complex, as in thwarting an attempt by employees of ill-repute who try to destroy a team member's good name, going back to our definition of intention, it is the evidenced "resolve" or "determination to" show care and concern that illuminates the mark of greatness.

"The challenge of leadership is to be strong but not rude; be kind, but not weak; be bold, but not a bully; be humble, but not timid; be proud, but not arrogant; have humor, but without folly."

JIM ROHN

SECTION 2

The "Love Connection"

LEADERSHIP AND ITS CONNECTION TO LOVE

I am not certain that people think about how they are going to "love" their team members when they become leaders. Love is most often discussed in the eros or philia terms. **Eros** love is the passionate type of love. When we have strong feelings that are sensual in nature, we are said to have an eros type of love.

Philia, the love that we have for friends or equals, is another type of love. When we have the philia type of love, it happens because we have something in common with the other person, in most instances. For example, I have some friends from my dance community. We became friends because we have the love of dance in common. From there, grew other commonalities. However, the base of our friendship rests in our enjoyment of dancing. You may have established friendships at work because you share the same boss or the same department. From there, you establish that there are other things that you enjoy, the same sports team, or the same types of food, or you have a similar sense of humor. These are a few things that can create that sense of philia, or brotherly love, for another person.

A less commonly discussed type of love is **storge**. This is the type of love that parents have for their children. While I have seen parents grow weary of their children, and, in some cases, distance themselves from them, particularly when they reach adulthood, it is rare that we would hear those parents deny the love that they have for their children. In fact, if asked the question, "Do you love your son"? or "Do you love your daughter"? The answer would be, "Of course, I do. That is my son/daughter." With storge love, that relationship is all that it takes. The parent-to-child bond is all that is needed for love to exist.

The type of love that leaders need to exhibit, however, is none of the aforementioned. The love that leaders must demonstrate to their team members is grounded in sacrifice and selflessness. This love is called **agape**.

Agape Love in Leadership

What is agape love? Agape, pronounced **ah-GAHP-ee,** is the name of the Greek goddess of love in mythology. Agape love is the love of humankind. Its requirement for delivery is, simply, that the person is human. When agape love is defined, words like sacrificial, selfless, and forgiving, are often used.

When in the role of leadership, we must build working relationships with people who have personality differences, race differences, different ethnicities, different genders, different ideologies derived from a diverse set of lived experiences, and more. When making decisions about what is best for the team, personal feelings about these factors are to become nil. When leading from a place of agape love, your feelings are not the driver of your decisions. This requires sacrifice so that you may think about what is in the best interest of the members of your team and make your decisions accordingly. In the documentary that I mentioned previously, The Playbook: A Coach's Rules for Life, Doc Rivers, one of the most successful NBA coaches in history, said that when he makes a decision, he may not like it, his players may not like it, but the choice will be made if it's in the best interest of the team. This is sacrificial love. This is agape love.

Agape Love as an Intentional Leader

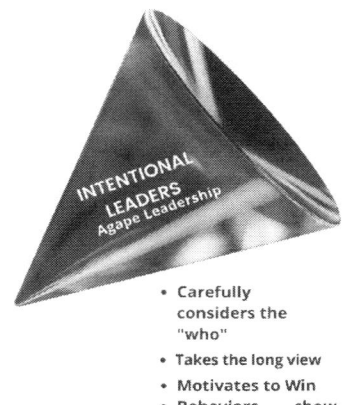

INTENTIONAL LEADERS
Agape Leadership

- Carefully considers the "who"
- Takes the long view
- Motivates to Win
- Behaviors show that you matter

One leader who has come to the forefront more recently and seems to demonstrate agape love as an intentional leader is "Coach Prime," Deion Sanders, the head football coach of Jackson State University. Coach Prime took a pay cut to help the University fund the new locker room for the players. When asked why he did that, he said, "Because they deserve it." The "deserve" that he meant was not because they had won several games, and this was their reward. Rather, it was because they were human beings who deserved the best. This is selfless care and concern for others, agape love.

As an intentional leader, he: demonstrated a behavior that showed that they matter, carefully considered who would be impacted, motivated the team to take their game to the next level, and took the long view, recognizing that this short-term financial sacrifice would reap long-term gains for the players and the school.

His expression of agape love for his team as an intentional leader has placed Jackson State University in a spotlight that is unmatched in recent years. The most important thing to note is that the recognition grew organically from his authentic way of leading his team with love...agape love.

It is impossible to be an intentional leader and not be one who operates from a place of agape love.

Leading intentionally requires that we be selfless in our determination and resolve to do what is in the best interests of our teams. As we "carefully consider the 'who," the decision we make cannot be centered around who we like better, or who we think will shine, but not outshine, us. Too often, I have heard of leaders who do not want to let a team member take an assignment for fear that the person may get more accolades than them. This comes from a place of insecurity and is selfish. A leader who is intentional and is leading from the place of agape love, makes the selection based on objective factors that they believe will create the best result for the team, not for them as a leader or the person who is chosen (although both may be by-products of the decision).

When an intentional leader "takes the long view" and uses systems thinking in planning and strategizing, sacrifices are often a part of the decision-making process. Thinking sacrificially may mean that costs may need to be cut in an area of enjoyment. Team travel or the annual group outing may need to be reduced so that the team may reap more bonuses at the start of the year. An intentional leader may decide to work more weekends to learn a new system or a new process that is going to help the team be better prepared. These are just two of the sacrifices that an intentional leader who is operating from a place of agape love may make.

As a motivator, an intentional leader exercises agape love when he or she "keeps no record of wrongs." When leaders harbor grudges for mistakes that a team member makes or for an uncomfortable conversation, it can be de-motivating for the team. A leader who exercises agape love, separates the person from the problem, manages the latter and focuses on inspiring and motivating the team member to be better in the future.

Being a leader who exercises agape love does not suggest that there will be no trying times. Instead, it suggests that the leader will exercise human kindness in working through challenges as they arise.

Doc Rivers, Dawn Staley and Coach Prime, Deion Sanders, as well as Jose' Mourinho, renowned football (soccer) coach, also highlighted in The Playbook: A Coach's Rules for Life, demonstrated behaviors that showed the teammates mattered. Coach Mourinho mentioned that he had been suspended because of an incident where he violated one of the rules. The suspension came amid a championship run for his team.

He was not allowed to be in the locker room nor the stadium. He believed, however, that his team needed him. Because of this, he went against the rules and hid himself in the locker room so that he could be there for his team at half-time. Where did he hide? He hid himself in the garbage can! Not only could he have been caught, but he could also have been dumped with the trash!

The thought of becoming a part of the rubble was not what was paramount to him, however. What mattered most to him was that he be there for his team. For them, he was willing to sacrifice his reputation, his standing, and his safety. Leaders like him, and the others mentioned earlier, are fantastic examples of what it means to be an intentional leader, one who operates from the place of agape love.

Agape Love-A Basis of Servant Leadership

Intentional leaders are servant leaders. Servant leaders demonstrate agape love.

Before delving more deeply into these statements, let us look at what a servant leader is.

The term servant leadership like the word "intention" is tossed around quite frequently in the professional development space. It has a very warm feel, yet I tend to believe that the qualities of servant leadership are not actualized as often as the term is mentioned, leaving team members, well...unserved.

So that we ensure that you have a complete understanding of what is asked of a person who deems to be a servant leader, we researched the term's etymology.

Robert Greenleaf in his book, "The Servant as Leader" introduced the term servant leadership. As Mr. Greenleaf stated, the questions that one should ask if seeking to become a servant leader are," "Do those served grow as persons? Do they, while being served, become healthier, wiser, freer, more autonomous, more likely themselves to become servants? (Wikipedia, 2022)

Intentional leaders, servant leaders, do not operate from a place of what they can take, but rather, they operate from a place of what they are able to give. They give help. They give advice. They provide vision. They provide motivation. They give encouragement. They assist in development. They provide stewardship, of time and resources. All these things and more are rooted in their desire to lead ... with selfless and sacrificial LOVE, AGAPE LOVE.

Therefore, when considering agape love as a basis for servant leadership, I submit that one is not separate from the other. When a leader is in the position of service it involves selflessness and sacrifice. It requires a decrease in the pursuit of personal gain for the more fulfilling pursuit of corporate achievement. Servant leadership and agape love are not mutually exclusive. They are akin.

SECTION 3

The Languages of Agape Leadership

The Languages of Agape Leadership

How will team members know that their leader is speaking the language of agape? How will a leader speak the language of agape as he/she leads with intention?

When we use the term language, we are going beyond what comes from the mouth. Language means, "the principal method of human communication, consisting of words used in a structured and conventional way and conveyed by speech, writing, or gesture."[3] In fact, the languages that we will focus are more related to gestures, or

---
[3] Language. N.d. Oxford languages. https://www.google.com/search?q=language+definition

behaviors, than they are to words. Why is that? The languages of agape leadership focus on behaviors because, as the adage states, "Actions speak louder than words." When leaders say that they support their teams, but do not demonstrate it with their actions, dissonance happens. There is a disconnect and confusion ensues.

In the words of my Pastor, "Your audio and video do not match!" A disconnect between words and actions is what creates an atmosphere of distrust. As intentional leaders, trust and credibility are foundational. If the team cannot trust their leader, the leader has no chance of being able to foster the atmosphere necessary for success.

When looking at the communication pie, words only account for 7% of our language. Thirty-eight percent of our communication is tone of voice, and the BIGGEST part of our communication, 55% is our BODY LANGUAGE! It is our physiology, the way our body functions, which contributes most to language being understood. In other words, the languages of agape come to life, not by what we say...but by what we do.

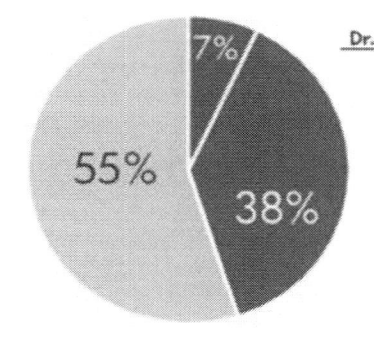

Dr. Albert Mehrabian's 7-38-55% Rule

Elements of Personal Communication
- 7% spoken words
- 38% voice, tone
- 55% body language

For purposes of AGAPE: The Language of Intentional Leadership, we will highlight the seven key languages of an agape leader, a servant leader. When leading with intention to be sacrificial and selfless, these are the behaviors, the body language that you will exude. At the end of this book, please take the self-assessment. This will give you an idea of the agape language(s) that you demonstrate most organically.

Is it possible to demonstrate all of them? Sure, it is. However, there will be some that come to you most naturally. As you grow in your leadership journey you will find it easier to draw on behaviors more readily. As I heard one great leader say, "It's like building a muscle." As those of us who are workout aficionados know, the more we exercise, the stronger we become. If we do enough push-ups, eventually we do not have to flex our arms for our muscles to show. People see them, even when they are covered. The same applies to the languages of agape leadership. The more we build the muscles of agape leadership, the more the behaviors will show. They will be undeniable, and your teams will be top tier!

What are the Languages of Agape Leadership?

The languages of Agape Leadership are:

- **Ambassador** of Forgiveness

- **Carrier** of Ethics

- **Team Leader** of Tenacity

- **Caretaker** of Temperance

- **Steward** of THE SHIP

- Relentless **Visionary**

- **Not Beyond Approach**

Seven represents the number of completion for those who are Biblical scholars, and these seven perfectly represent the behaviors of sacrificial, selfless love that intentional leaders need to demonstrate.

As we explore each one, begin to think about how well you are exhibiting the language as you lead yourself and others. Remember, this is about building the muscles of agape leadership. Some may be stronger than others, at first. However, as you continue to exercise them, you will develop into a beautiful body of leadership.

AGAPE

Agape Leadership Language

#1:

Ambassador of Forgiveness

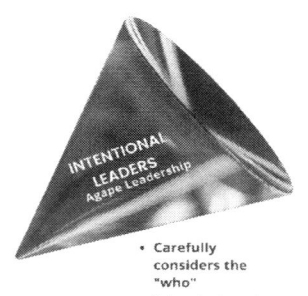

INTENTIONAL LEADERS
Agape Leadership

- Carefully considers the "who"
- Takes the long view
- Motivates to Win
- Behaviors show that you matter

Agape Leadership Language #1:

Ambassador of Forgiveness

In the spirit of leadership, where does forgiveness take its place? Everywhere. As leaders, there will be times when your team members betray you, do not perform to the level that you expect, say things behind your back that may or may not be true...the list can be endless. There will also be times when your peers will do the same. There may even be times when the people who lead you do things that warrant forgiveness to move forward.

In agape leadership, being an ambassador for forgiveness is necessary. Forgiveness requires that you become selfless. The place to begin becoming selfless is through communication with the party(ies) that wronged you. Seeking to reach a place of understanding is a critical first step toward forgiveness. It sets the stage for a broader awareness of the factors on both sides that led to the negative situation. As you work through understanding better, an ambassador of forgiveness makes a conscious decision to lay aside personal feelings. It is said that one must separate the person from the problem when seeking resolution to a dispute. If one can focus on the problem and preserve the relationship with the person, a greater win can result.

As leaders, there may be times that reaching an amicable resolution is not possible. As an ambassador of forgiveness, the agape leader resists the urge to hold grudges and create a negative environment because of the situation. Instead, the leader chooses to forgive, leave the matter in its place, and do what is needed to properly close the issue. Is this easy? It can be. It takes building of the forgiveness muscle.

As leaders, we are required to get out of our own way to give way to the best interests of the organization and the team. Carrying the weight of those who have wronged you can become a heavy burden in the way of this responsibility.

Being an ambassador of forgiveness does not mean that you are expected to let team members behave badly, nor does it mean that you let peers and other levels of leadership disrespect you or treat you unkindly. It means that you manage each moment of discourse as it comes and remain focused on resolving the problem.

Now, if the person IS the problem, then, "If you cannot change the person, CHANGE the person." The best place for some people will be outside of the employ of the company. Forgive them and help them to get freed to their next opportunity. Selah.

"Forgiveness is not an occasional act, it is a constant attitude."

DR. MARTIN LUTHER KING, JR.

Agape Leadership Language #2:

Carrier of Ethics

INTENTIONAL LEADERS
Agape Leadership

- Carefully considers the "who"
- Takes the long view
- Motivates to Win
- Behaviors show that you matter

Agape Leadership Language #2: Carrier of Ethics

Would you tell the truth about something that you did not do correctly, even if it meant you would be in trouble on your job? Would you tell the truth about something that you did incorrectly, even if it meant that you would be terminated?

While chewing on these big questions, here a few that your team members need to know:

- When you tell them that you will meet with them to help them through a concern, will you be there as you promised?

- When you say that you will help them to have a conversation with a leader in another department where they may want to work, will you?

- When they ask for your feedback, will you be honest, but not cynical?

- Will you develop your business acumen so that you can give them the best information possible?

The affirmative answer to these questions, and more, speak to whether you are a carrier of ethics.

In this world where we can take an innumerable number of pictures to capture the "perfect" one, and where we can edit clips of ourselves so that just the piece that makes us look the absolute best is seen, truth, in many ways, has become a delicacy. We can filter, lighten, darken, widen, and embellish images in so many ways it is virtually impossible to know what is really happening.

Even when we send text messages, we can send an exclamation point or bright smiley face when how we feel is quite the opposite.

Yet, as leaders, we are called to be ethical. We are called to be honest. Honesty has a direct impact on our credibility.

An agape leader is a carrier of ethics. The establishment of credibility happens as one delivers on the "the little things." As stated earlier, only 7% of our words account for our communication. Fifty-five percent of our communication lies in our body language, how we move, if and how we do what we say that we are going to do. If we fail to do what we say we are going to do, we are not carriers of ethics. To be a carrier of ethics, requires sacrifice, in some cases. It may be a sacrifice of your time, as in the case of feedback or help on a project. It may be a sacrifice of a resource, as in the case of yielding the way for a team member to talk to a colleague of yours for an opportunity that interests them. It may even be the sacrifice of your position, as in the case of telling the truth about something that you did wrong that may cost you your job. The last one is a big one. Hopefully, it is one that never happens to you. However, if you are a carrier of ethics, and you know that you have done something wrong, even if it may cost you your employment, tell the truth. The best way to remember what you have said, is to tell the truth. As someone said, "The truth crushed to the earth will still rise as truth."

Be intentional about being a carrier of ethics.

Agape Leadership Language

#3:

Team Leader of Tenacity

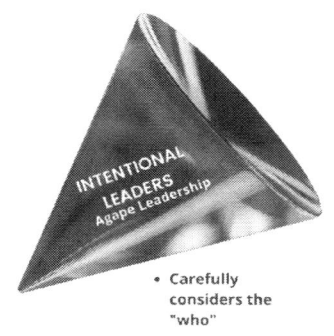

- Carefully considers the "who"
- Takes the long view
- Motivates to Win
- Behaviors show that you matter

Agape Leadership Language #3: Team Leader of Tenacity

To lead selflessly, one must be tenacious. Why? Because tenacity is the "carry-on-no-matter-what" muscle, and a selfless leader does just that. When one makes a commitment and sticks through until the end, even when the going gets tough and the way is not clear, it allows the other team members to be encouraged and motivated to be tenacious, as well.

Think for a moment, if you will, about a time when you had a difficult challenge and you did not know the way forward. You may have known that there was the "other side" of the mountain, but, in that moment, you could not see how you were going to arrive there. However, you kept going. You did one task, then the next, and the next. Eventually, the tasks became easier to complete and, almost immediately, the other side was right in front of you!

There was a time when I did not know how I was going to finish college. My father was sporadically paying tuition. My mom did not have money enough to send me, and my grades, at that time, were average, but not excellent. However, I was committed to graduating.

I remember looking into a mirror in our college apartment and saying to myself, "I will graduate. I do not know how, but I will," (now, I'd call this, as Pastor Michael Todd of Transformation Church in Oklahoma says, "Faith Talk"). I also decided that I was going to make the Dean's List. I had never made the Dean's List, but I believed that it was attainable.

To make the Dean's list I knew that I had to attack studying differently. I made the decision to rewrite my notes immediately following EVERY CLASS. I decided to write them immediately afterward because I knew that my brain would have a greater chance of solidifying the information if I did it then. I studied more and built a team of great friends, one of whom had the same major as me. We became so close we started choosing the same classes so that we could go to school together and study together. Having her made attending classes much more enjoyable. In fact, we are still friends to this day!

Did I make the Dean's List? Yes, I did. Not once, but twice. Did I graduate? Most certainly. It was the stick-to-it-iveness that helped me to reach the finish line, and just like climbing any mountain, as you are going up the hill, it feels difficult at first, but once you are close to the top, the way gets easier, and the air is fresher.

While this example is about my personal journey of tenacity, the same applies to leading others. When helping others, being a team leader of tenacity means that you decide to stick through a challenge with the team and carry them to the finish line, no matter what.

It may mean that you must give up time that you dedicated to something else so that you can be there for them. It may mean that you must encourage them to keep going, even though you do not see how they are going to succeed. When my son was learning to play the violin, every year he wanted to quit. His father and I would take him to our church, The Apostolic Church of God, each Saturday, and we would spend most of the day there from September through May. It was a sacrifice, especially given the fact that our son wanted to quit.

Something in my spirit said to keep going. The opportunity was too great not to continue. His dad and I could have opted for the "easier road" and let him give up on learning. We could have been selfish and said to ourselves, "Let us spend these weekends doing what we'd like to do since he seems not to care about this. We are spending gas and time each week. Let us just be selfish and allow him to quit!" As leaders of our household and our child this was not an option we chose, however.

Because we decided to be tenacious with him, he is now a Master Violinist, teaching, playing, and creating music for a living! His dad and I were "team leaders of tenacity" for our son.

When we are leading our teams, there may be times when you must "know when to fold 'em." The best option is not to move forward, but to retreat. Intuitive thinking will be your guide to lead you in the right direction for the time.

When the call is for tenacity, however, do not give up, do not retreat. Plan your work and work your plan. Lead your teams with tenacity. It is a gift that continues to give.

Agape Leadership Language #4:

Caretaker of Temperance

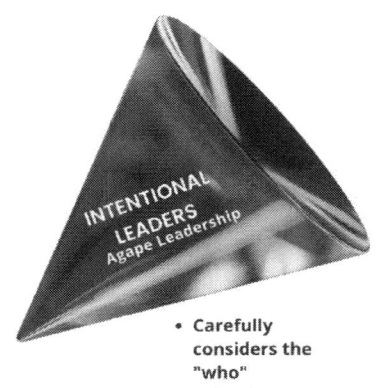

- Carefully considers the "who"
- Takes the long view
- Motivates to Win
- Behaviors show that you matter

Agape Leadership Language #4:

Caretaker of Temperance

When the "ship" gets unsteady, a leader's job is to steady it. When the leader is unnerved and lacks restraint it is difficult to create solutions that produce the best outcomes. Temperance, or moderation in action and feelings, happens when one looks at a situation or circumstance, and chooses response over reaction.

Reaction is typically quick in nature. Things that happen quickly rarely land in a moderate place. They tend to either take us to an extremely high place or to an exceptionally low place. Leaders who react instead of responding typically land at one of the poles.

Response happens in more of a slow-cook process. The event takes place. The circumstances are processed. A decision is made. This does not have to happen over a prolonged period, but it does happen through a series of moments in the brain. This is where one's emotional quotient score is derived.

Emotional quotient, or EQ, as Daniel Goleman, the chief

architect of EQ puts it, is the *sine qua non* of leadership. It is that essential thing.

In the brain are two almond shaped components called the amygdalae. When the amygdalae are triggered by moments of distress or eustress, a plethora of emotions from joy, anxiety, distress, excitement, depression, and exuberance can enter. The space between the feeling that arises from the emotional trigger and the person's reaction is a major part of one's emotional quotient.

Warren Bennis, a leading organizational consultant of his time and author of *"On Becoming a Leader,"* said of the importance of emotional intelligence, "Emotional intelligence, more than any other factor, more than I.Q. or expertise, accounts for 85% to 90% of success at work... I.Q. is a threshold competence. You need it, but it does not make you a star. Emotional intelligence can." (Warren G. Bennis, 2022)[4]

When a leader exercises temperance, the four components of emotional intelligence are working nicely together, leading to an

---

[4] Warren G. Bennis. (n.d.). AZQuotes.com. Retrieved November 13, 2022, from AZQuotes.com Web site: https://www.azquotes.com/quote/958856 **Chicago Style Citation**

emotionally intelligent response. First, self-awareness helps the leader to be in touch with how they are feeling in the moment. This skill is essential for knowing when to step forward and when to step away to step forward. Sometimes the best response in the moment is no response. Increasing self-awareness helps with this, or helps us with the second component, self-regulation. To be aware of what one is feeling and then to interrupt a reaction is a game-changer! It can mean the difference between winning the moment and winning the day. When we can self-regulate, we can win the day. The other half of the emotional quotient deals with how we manage others. Social awareness speaks to how well we can "temperature check" others. Going back to our definition of how 93% of communication is made of gestures, voice tone, and behaviors, one who is good at social awareness can read what is not said when deciding how to move forward in resolving a situation. Social regulation is the fourth quadrant. This relates to how you manage others. The ability to regulate is tied to your ability to influence. An intentional leader who operates with agape leadership will have a greater chance of being able to regulate others because he or she will be coming from the place of what is best for the team instead of what is best for them as leaders. As mentioned earlier in this book, that is how Doc Rivers leads.

A leader who is a caretaker of temperance has a high emotional quotient. This leader will behave in a way that chooses appropriate responses for the situation. This is not to say that everyone will respond in the same way to the same stimuli. It is saying that, given a set of circumstances, one with a high emotional quotient will demonstrate behaviors that show thought and mindfulness when making decisions.

If you would like to know more about emotional intelligence and your emotional quotient, go to our website at www.worldclasstraining.net/pd and connect to us to learn how you and your team may get stronger in this area.

Agape Leadership Language #5:

Relentless Visionary

- Carefully considers the "who"
- Takes the long view
- Motivates to Win
- Behaviors show that you matter

Agape Leadership Language #5:

Relentless Visionary

Let us take another look at our Intentional Leadership model:

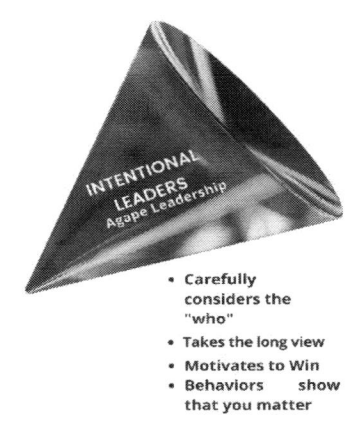

INTENTIONAL LEADERS
Agape Leadership

- Carefully considers the "who"
- Takes the long view
- Motivates to Win
- Behaviors show that you matter

The second bullet point, **takes the long view**, can only happen with a leader who is a visionary. An agape leader, one who demonstrates selfless, sacrificial care and concern for others, is a *relentless visionary*.

A relentless visionary always sees new opportunities and new possibilities for the team. As the organization shifts and changes, the goals and markers of success must be adjusted.

Think for a moment about when you are driving on a long-distance trip. The GPS is set for that location and has all the places that you will pass on the way embedded into the map. As the trip progresses, there may be an accident reported that causes a delay. Before you arrive at the accident, the GPS provides an update and tells you that you can take an alternate route (if available). It has seen virtually into the distance and helps you to adjust.

The same applies to the intentional leader as a relentless visionary. This person sees into the future of the organization and the team. As new initiatives are launched, new team members are added, or new structures and processes are put in place, the leader takes the long view and considers what the impacts of these changes are. Then the vision may be redirected to keep the team moving in the right direction.

Being relentless means that the visionary must not be shy about charting the course for the team. The vision must be laid consistently and shared broadly. If the visionary does not share where he or she would like for the team to land with those who will help get there, he cannot be upset when there is either misalignment or misdirection.

One must be intentional, resolved or determined, to have a vision, write the vision and communicate it plainly.

"Good business leaders create a vision, articulate the vision, passionately own the vision and relentlessly drive it to completion"

JACK WELCH.

Agape Leadership Language #6:

Never Beyond Approach

INTENTIONAL LEADERS
Agape Leadership

- Carefully considers the "who"
- Takes the long view
- Motivates to Win
- Behaviors show that you matter

Agape Leadership Language #6:

Never Beyond Approach

To be selfless, putting the needs of the team above one's own is essential. Also, being a good listener is important. A leader's primary responsibility is to be in service to others. Listening, serving, and considering the needs of the team requires being approachable.

There is an adage that states, "one does not care how much you know until they know how much you care." When we look at the intentional leadership model that has as one of its principles that an intentional leader "demonstrates behaviors that show you matter," the best way that this can manifest itself is for the leader to be easily approachable.

Each team member has his or her own personality, set of circumstances and needs. As a leader, it is necessary to produce corporate results while working through these individual idiosyncrasies. When training a team of leaders in Hartford, CT a few years ago, one of the leaders looked at me and said, "It's like we're psychologists." I paused and replied, "In some ways, you are absolutely correct." Leaders are not formally trained in psychology, in most cases. However, the longer they are in position the more they become aware of the need to work with the minds of their team members so that they can achieve positive outcomes. To do this, approachability is key.

Mentioned earlier in this book, one of my best leaders, Dion, earned the title because he was approachable. He made sure to speak to each of us in the morning when he arrived at work. When I had a concern with another team member, I felt extremely comfortable approaching him to share my concern. Why? Because he demonstrated that I mattered.

Let me caution you that being approachable does not equate to being always available. It also does not mean that the leader should not expect that the rules of the organization and team are followed. Sometimes team members make the error of mistaking kindness for weakness. The two are mutually exclusive. It is necessary to set boundaries and disallow relationships that are too fraternizing. I have often said to leaders that they should, "Be friendly, but be careful who they call their friend."

Being approachable is about setting an atmosphere that breeds comfort from the team in working together towards a strong corporate culture. It is about recognizing and operating intentionally from the role of servant leadership. It is about selfless, sacrificial care and concern for others. It is about agape.

Agape Leadership Language

#7:

Steward of "The Ship"

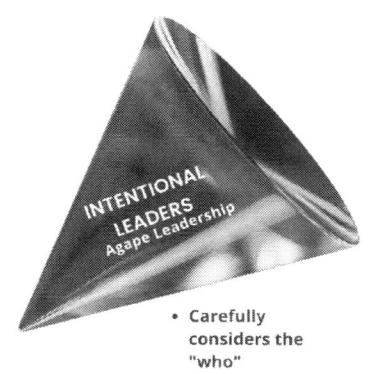

INTENTIONAL LEADERS
Agape Leadership

- Carefully considers the "who"
- Takes the long view
- Motivates to Win
- Behaviors show that you matter

Agape Leadership Language #7:

Steward of "The Ship"

Being a steward is about being a careful watch person. An agape leader is a watch person over many aspects of their leadership.

The first area that must be stewarded is relationship. While some may think about financial resources when thinking about stewarding, leaders must be good stewards of their relationships. Connections are important to increasing influence. As leaders grow in their role, they will recognize that the relationship pool may not be as vast, but the quality of the relationships will be richer. This is because they are built over longer periods of time, or after going through moments of significance together. No matter the reason, leaders find that they want to hold on to solid comrades and constituents.

Stewarding time is another critical area for great leadership. If I have a dollar and give it to you today, I can potentially get it returned to me tomorrow. If I give you a minute, it is gone forever. This statement is true and particularly important. As a leader, the way time is spent can be the difference between winning and losing. Think about your favorite sport. The score can be close for most of the game. There can be several possession and lead changes. However, when the clock strikes zero, the only thing that matters is the team that is ahead at the end. When the clock runs out, time is up...period. Similarly, in an organization if we are late attending meetings, we can miss the one piece of information that was necessary to our jobs. If we allow others to eat up our day with trivial matters, we run short on time needed to complete larger, more significant tasks and projects. Lacking organization can lead to time spent looking for documentation or figuring out how to spend the day. These are all time wasters and not representative of good stewardship of time.

Finally, yes, stewarding money well is critical. Intentional leaders, agape leaders, are focused on careful consideration of who and where funds are being allocated. For many leaders, how they manage financial resources is a performance management indicator. This is because these numbers can have a direct impact on the company's profitability, and even bonuses, at the end of the year.

SECTION 4

The Distinctions

The Distinctions

When leading with the agape love languages, the distinctions are vastly different from those who do not. The culture of your organization can experience seismic shifts in a positive direction when implemented continuously. Eventually, the language becomes a part of the organization's DNA.

Additionally, intentional leadership values reveal themselves seamlessly. It becomes difficult, in fact, to exhibit the language of agape leadership and not also be demonstrating intentional leadership.

Let us explore a few of the distinctions of the agape love language leader.

Distinction #1: Heightened Team Comradery

The leader who exhibits these traits will have a heightened sense of team comradery. People want to work for leaders who are tempered, ethical, forgiving, tenacious, great visionaries and stewards of time and resources. The more that leaders work to bring forward these traits daily with their team, the more they will begin to feel and move like a cohesive unit. Trust is built and sensitivities to what is important to each other becomes greater. This distinction is one of the most important.

Distinction #2: Stronger Results

Think, for a moment, about those for whom we have eros, philia or storge love. When we have this type of love for someone, we tend to go the extra mile. We will take more time communicating, or spend more time at an event, or assisting, as is the case with storge love. We may spend more money on the person if we feel one of these types of love. The underlying reason for any of these behaviors is to produce strong relationship results.

The same concept applies to demonstrating agape love behaviors. Demonstrating the tenants described here will produce stronger results for the team. It goes back to the principle that, "They do not care how much you know, until they know how much you care." Once the team believes that you care, not about the company, but about them, they will be driven to produce more which will result in stronger results. Leaders must operate from the spirit of Ubuntu, the southern African term, which when translated means, "I am because we are." When leaders operate from the place of Ubuntu, then they will work to help each team member be his or her best individually so that the team can succeed collectively, or in other words, "the whole becomes greater than the sum of its parts."

Distinction #3: The Minimization of Stress

You may ask, "How does stress decrease when using these principles?" I am glad that you asked. Let me explain.

When we think about some of the big causes of stress in leadership, they arise from one of a few areas: 1) someone has wronged the leader and they are upset with that person, 2) too many projects are being presented, causing stress and confusion in the mind of the leader, and 3) the leader has been dishonest and is concerned that their dishonesty will be revealed.

Taking the first possibility, being wronged, leaders who are short on forgiveness will carry around the baggage of what was done to them, leading to stress and difficulty. However, leaders who can move past the moment, or become Ambassadors of Forgiveness, and separate the problem from the person will have less moments of stress. This does not mean that the leader does not need to be mindful of what occurred, but rather, the leader does not create a debilitating situation because of it.

In the second scenario, multiple projects with multiple deadlines can present stress-filled days. One may feel as if they can never get everything done or that they are under-performing because they are being pulled in too many directions. Enter the agape love languages. By first being a "Steward of The SHIP," the leader will plan out the time and the resources, both human and tactical, that can help to accomplish the goals. Coupling this with being a "Team Leader of Tenacity" and a "Caretaker of Temperance" will lower stress and produce outcomes that the whole team can celebrate because the whole team played a role in the projects' completion.

Distinction #4: The "Light" is Undeniable

There is a light that shines from certain people when they enter a space. Something about their appearance lets everyone within proximity to them have a sense that this moment is going to be filled with more. The more may be kindness, gentleness, excitement, progression, brilliance, or care, as examples. Because of this sense that more is about to happen, however, there is a leaning into what is being presented. This light illuminates authentically from the ones who carry it. It cannot be turned on, and it does not turn off. The reason that this light is so organically bright is because it comes from a place of love.

Marianne Williamson, the famous author, and poet wrote in her book" A *Return to Love*" about Our Deepest Fear. This piece of written work is one of the most powerful about the strength that we all have when we choose to live in our light.

She wrote, "*Our deepest fear is not that we are inadequate. Our deepest fear is that we are powerful beyond measure. It is our light, not our darkness that most frightens us. We ask ourselves, Who am I to be brilliant, gorgeous, talented, fabulous? Actually, who are you not to be? You are a child of God. Your playing small does not serve the world. There is nothing enlightened about shrinking so that other people won't feel insecure around you. We are all meant to shine, as children do. We were born to make manifest the glory of God that is within us. It's not just in some of us; it's in everyone. And as we let our own light shine, we unconsciously give other people permission to do the same. As we are liberated from our own fear, our presence automatically liberates others."[5]*

And so, it is. When we choose to lead from a place of agape love, it is going to reveal a light that is undeniable. Those who lead with integrity, forgiveness, temperance, vision, stewardship, tenacity, and are approachable walk different. It is like how we drive when we know the exact location we are heading toward as opposed to when we are searching for an address. We tend to drive more tentatively because we are unsure.

---

[5] (Williamson, 1996)

When you lead with these tools, you may not have all the answers all the time. You will, however, have assurance. This is the assurance that you are working in the best interests of those you have been called to serve. When this is your driver, your light is undeniable.

A Few Final Thoughts

A Closing Love Letter

Dear Leaders:

Developing the language of Intentional Leadership, agape, may come with growing pains. For instance, there will be team members who will do things that may seem unforgivable. You will have to continue a working relationship, although you have determined that they are not to be trusted. There may be other instances where you are riddled with trying circumstances that challenge your temperance. In fact, for each of the seven languages, opposition in some form or another will exist at some point.

When these challenges arise, remember that when a language has been practiced enough, it becomes the initial way that you communicate. For those of us who use English as our native tongue, whenever we seek to communicate, we naturally begin speaking in English. The same rule applies here. When you develop a deep commitment to using the behaviors found in this book, it will become second nature for you. You will know in that moment of leadership distress that you have sprung forth with a new level of self and leadership proficiency.

Getting to this place may not be easy, but it will most definitely be worth it.

Shine your light with Intentional Leadership.

Shine your light with selfless, sacrificial care and concern for others.

Shine your light with the language of **AGAPE**.

Love Always,

Dawn

BONUS:

What's Your Primary Agape Leadership Language?

Join in on the fun and take the quiz to determine which agape leadership language is most organic for you. Simply scan the QR Code below.

When you finish, share your results with your friends and colleagues and see if they agree.

Lastly, send us a quick video of you telling us your result and share why you believe that it is or is not accurate. Make it fun! You just may see yourself on a reel!

AGAPE

FOR YOUR REFLECTION

Note's Pages

Dawn Marie Morris

AGAPE

Dawn Marie Morris

AGAPE

Dawn Marie Morris

AGAPE

Dawn Marie Morris

AGAPE

AGAPE

Dawn Marie Morris

AGAPE

ABOUT DAWN MARIE MORRIS

Dawn Marie Morris, Chief Training Officer of The World Class Training Institute, Inc., is the author of WWBD-What Would Barack Do? -Inspiring Presidential Tools for the Leader in You and is a professional development training leader and experienced career readiness expert of over 15 years. Ms. Morris has facilitated to audiences across this country on leadership and professional development. Her experiences include Fortune 500 companies, institutions of higher education and non-profit arenas. Specifically, her work has been recognized as having largely contributed to the ability for leadership at one Fortune 500 company to become some of the best in the business during her training tenure.

Dawn is the creator of Intentional Leadership-Leading in 3-D, a unique training experience that causes professionals to think more deeply about their roles as leaders, the strengths, and desires of their team members, and how thinking systematically creates an organization of powerful synergy. Her corporate training experience and business client list includes: Wintrust Bank, Dick's Sporting Goods, Lee Company, United Way of Greensboro, N.C., Tennessee State University, University of Pittsburgh, College of Charleston, St. Mary's College in Texas, and Tusculum College, to name a few.

A graduate of Howard University in Washington, D. C. with a BBA-Marketing and having continued her studies in the Master of Arts-Training and Communication program at Governors State University in Illinois, Ms. Morris is a strong proponent of quality education. Dawn was featured in Canvas Rebel Magazine in November 2022 and in the November 2021 issue of The Nashville Voyager as a "Hidden Gem". Ms. Morris is a repeat contributor for Emerging Leaders magazine, a collaborative publication that provides insight and guidance to help those in middle to executive level management. Dawn is a highly energetic and engaging speaker. She makes sure to combine knowledge of the topic, creativity in design and articulation in delivery so that her audiences are left educated, entertained, and inspired.

Dawn is a mother of one, Brian Keith Cooper II, and resides in Nashville, TN.

Connect to us for all of your leadershipdevelopment needs:

615-716-9990

www.worldclasstraining.net

Facebook, Instagram, Linked In and YouTube:

The World Class Training Institute

Connect to Dawn on IG at

iam.dawn.marie

Printed in Great Britain
by Amazon

ef548043-fa1d-4b5e-8fc1-bd218b9639c6R01